retro
Cocktails

shake it baby!

Kate Moseley

retro
Cocktails
shake it baby!

Kate Moseley

MQP

Published by MQ Publications Limited
12 The Ivories
6-8 Northampton Street
London N1 2HY
Tel: +44 (0)20 7359 2244
Fax: +44 (0)20 7359 1616
email: mail@mqpublications.com
website: www.mqpublications.com

Text Copyright © 2002 Kate Moseley
Photography: Chris Alack
Styling: Sue Radcliffe
Design: Lindsey Johns, Design Revolution
Editor: Leanne Bryan

ISBN: 1-84072-460-9

10 9 8 7 6 5 4 3 2

Printed and bound in China

contents

5

Equipment

Cocktail shaker

There are several types of cocktail shaker to choose from, but the two most common are the standard and the Boston. The standard usually comes in chrome but can be made from toughened plastic. The base, also known as the "can," resembles a tall, cone-shaped tumbler. It has a tight fitting funnel top with built-in strainer holes on which the cap fits snugly. The Boston shaker comprises a tall metal beaker and a plain glass beaker which fits tightly inside it. The metal beaker has a pouring hole, often with a built-in strainer and cap. The glass beaker can also be used as a mixing glass. Both are efficient and easy to keep clean.

Cocktail Strainer

The Boston shaker is used in conjunction with a cocktail- or "Hawthorne" strainer. This comes in two parts: a frame, and an edge of wire coil to prevent spillage. The protruding prongs balance on the rim of the cocktail shaker. The strainer (inserted inside the shaker) is held firmly and the liquid is poured out between the prongs. Perforations allow the liquid to pass through without the ice falling into the glass. For even finer straining, use a fine mesh sieve or a tea strainer held just above the glass.

Citrus Zester

A small tool usually having a line of five small rings on the top set at an angle. These are, in fact, quite sharp and when held firmly against the skin of the citrus fruit and dragged downward, or towards you, will form fine lines of zest.

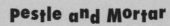

Pestle and Mortar

A mortar is a bowl-like vessel made of hard material, usually ceramic or marble, that is used for crushing or grounding ingredients with the pestle—a club-shaped, handheld tool. Avoid using wooden mortars which taint easily when used with wet ingredients and can be unhygenic.

Citrus Juicer

Freshly squeezed lemon, orange, and lime are far superior to anything ready prepared in a bottle. Electric spinning juicers are ideal for making big batches, but be careful not to overdo it and grind the pith as well which makes the juice, and so the drink, bitter. A simple stainless steel or glass lemon squeezer is fine for the job. Make sure it has a good lip for catching the juice and enough "teeth" or a good strainer to catch the pips. You'll get more juice from your fruit if you roll the fruit first on your bar chopping board with the palm of your hand, applying gentle pressure. When you cut the fruit in half the juice should be released more easily. Heating whole or halved fruit for a few seconds in a dish in the microwave will also make them juicier, but watch out as the fruit and juice will be warm. Although juice extraction seems tedious, the flavor in the cocktail makes it all worthwhile. Bottled or canned juices can be too sweet or contain preservatives that taint the flavor. If fresh juice makes the drink too sharp, add a little sugar syrup.

Stirring Rod

A glass stick used for stirring drinks with ice in the mixing glass. Especially useful for mixing carbonated cocktails and martinis.

Bar Spoon

The classic bar spoon has a long, handle (about 10 inches/ 25cm), with an oval or teardrop shaped bowl. It can be used as a spoon measure (slightly larger than the average teaspoon) as well as for stirring drinks and muddling ingredients. The best ones have a twisted stem (or barley/spiral effect) and a flat end to prevent them from slipping. They are easier to grip than their smooth-stemmed counterparts.

Muddler

This is a short, rounded, wooden "baton," similar to a pestle but with a flat end. It is used to mash sugar and Angostura bitters, or sugar and fresh mint, until the sugar dissolves. It may also be used for crushing fruit in a glass by pushing down on it with a twisting action, or for crushing ice cubes. Alternatively, use a pestle and mortar (see opposite), the end of a small rolling pin in a bowl, or the heel of a mixing spoon.

Jigger and Pony

The standard measure for ingredients is known as a "jigger" and holds 1½fl oz US/45ml. Another standard measure is a "pony" which measures 2 tablespoons or 1fl oz US/30ml. Measures are available in other sizes and are often called "shots." A shot, ideally, is 1fl oz US/30ml. If you don't have a measure, a standard liqueur glass will be fine to use. In fact, anything can be used as a measure as long as it is used consistently throughout the recipe to keep the proportions right. A clean medicine measure, the cap off a bottle, or half an egg cup are other suggestions.

Measuring spoons

Measuring spoons come in sets of ⅙fl oz US, ⅓fl oz US and ½fl oz US (5ml,10ml and 15ml) in stainless steel or plastic.

Ice Cream Scoop

If you fancy serving ice cream or sorbet cocktails, a metal scoop is the best to use because it's quick and easy to clean. Just dip it in hot water before scooping the ice cream into the drink. Always put the ice cream straight back into the freezer after taking the scoops.

Chopping board and fruit knife

A small wooden board and sharp stainless knife are required for cutting and preparing fruit for garnishing.

Mixing glass

A straight, plain, glass pitcher with a lip for pouring, used to chill a cocktail as quickly as possible. It should take be large enough to take 1½ pints US (24fl oz US/750ml) of fluid. Don't be tempted to buy a colored or patterned glass pitcher—a clear mixing glass will allow you to see if any "foreign bodies" have fallen into the cocktail by mistake. Alternatives include a straight water pitcher, a clear glass bottle, a measuring pitcher, or the glass beaker from a Boston shaker.

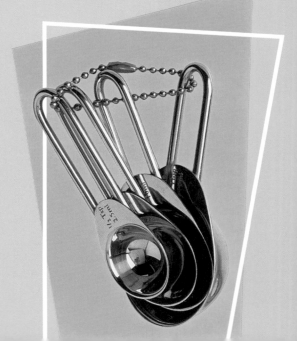

Ice Bucket

The better the ice bucket is insulated, the longer the ice will last. Keep the lid on and use a good pair of tongs to lift the ice out.

Paring Knife

A small sharp knife used for taking a thin layer of citrus peel in strands, or parings, from the fruit. Also useful for cutting wedges and other fruit shapes.

Canelle knife

A small tool with a grooved attachment on top used to cut citrus spirals. Hold this against the fruit and steadily drag it round the fruit to get a spiral of peel, thicker and more robust than when using a zester.

Cocktail sticks

Small wooden or plastic sticks of varying colors, plain or with decorative ends, are used to spear maraschino cherries, olives, small onions, or slices of fruit for garnishing cocktails. Plastic sticks can be reused after sterilization, whereas the wooden variety should be thrown away.

Blender/Liquidizer

Only use a domestic food blender if it is equipped to cope with crushing ice. If not, consider investing in a commercial blender. It is still preferable to use cracked or crushed ice as this will save wear and tear on the blender's blades and motor. A good blender should have several speeds or action settings, a goblet made of heavy-duty glass, plastic, or stainless steel, and detachable blades to enable thorough cleaning. (Use a bottlebrush for safety and speed when cleaning the blades.) When using the blender to make cocktails, measure in the ingredients, then add crushed ice and start the machine on slow speed, building up speed to produce a smooth, even consistency. Strain into a glass and serve immediately.

Glamorous Glassware

Highball glass

A clear, simple, tall glass used for any drink containing alcohol and a mixer and served with ice, such as gin and tonic or a Harvey Wallbanger.

Brandy snifter

Short stemmed with a large balloon-like bowl. Traditionally used for brandy and some liqueurs. The bulbous cup is designed to let the hand warm the drink while the cup shape wafts the tantalizing aroma to your nose. Though the glass is large in volume, only pour in a couple of ounces of brandy at a time.

Collins glass

Taller and thinner than the highball, the Collins glass is often frosted or pebbled with a smooth rim. Perfect for serving a Tom Collins, this glass is also used for fizzes and tropical drinks.

Champagne flute

This tall, elegant glass is an excellent way to serve champagne, as it both showcases the wine's bouquet while retaining the bubbles for longer due to its small surface area.

Old-fashioned glass

Also known as tumbler, lowball, whiskey or rocks glass. Short, broad, flat-bottomed glass, essential for serving any drink "on the rocks" (with ice).

Boston glass

Tall, slightly conical highball glass.

Cocktail glass

Classic, stemmed glass, often referred to as a "Martini" glass. Used for serving drinks "straight up" (without ice), the slender stem of the cocktail glass prevents the heat of your hand from warming the contents as you sip.

Toddy glass

Short heatproof glass used to serve toddies made of liquor, hot water, and spices.

Wineglass

The white wineglass is slightly smaller than the red wineglass, which has a rounder, more balloon-like shape.

Margarita glass

Larger and rounder than the traditional cocktail glass, the Margarita has a unique double bowl. Used for Margaritas and Daiquiris.

Irish coffee glass

Thick, heatproof glass with foot, short stem, and glass handle used for serving hot coffee mixed with a liqueur.

Champagne saucer

Commonly used for serving champagne, but this elegant glass allows the bubbles and bouquet of the drink to escape faster than the champagne flute.

Shot glass

A tiny glass, often called a "jigger" used for measuring and serving short drinks with a high alcohol content called "shooters."

Goblet

Short, bowl-shaped glass with foot and short stem.

Tricks of the Trade

Sugar Syrup

Some cocktails taste better with a little added sweetness to counteract the "sour" of fresh fruit juice. Try sprinkling a sugar cube with Angostura bitters, placing it in a glass and stirring (see Classic Champagne Cocktail, page 52). Alternatively, bruise sugar and fresh fruit or mint leaves with a muddler to make a paste, which can be added to the cocktail.

As granulated sugar doesn't dissolve easily in cold drinks, you may prefer to use "simple syrup" or "sirop de gomme," which can be bought ready made and comes in a variety of flavors including almond (orgeat) coconut, cassis, framboise, grenadine, and vanilla.

Sugar syrup is easily made by measuring a ratio of two parts granulated sugar to one part water into a pan. Stir over a gentle heat then bring to the boil for 3–5 minutes. The longer you boil it, the more concentrated it will become. Cool, then pour into a bottle and refrigerate. Sugar syrup should keep for a couple of months.

For variation, flavor the syrup with spices (for example cinnamon sticks, star anise, or fresh root ginger), lemongrass, or lime leaves.

Cream Cocktails

Rich and creamy, these cocktails were traditionally served at the end of a meal. These days, if you feel like one, any time is fine! Cream will mix with most liqueurs and can mask the harshness of alcohol, leaving a drink smooth enough to slide easily down the throat. Always use heavy cream to give the cocktail enough body. Be aware that the action of acid from fruit juices can react with the cream and make it look, and possibly taste, curdled if it is left to stand. For this reason it is important to serve the cocktail as soon as it has been made. Always keep the cream refrigerated and wash the bar equipment thoroughly after making cream cocktails.

Layering Pousse-Café

The pousse-café is a multi-colored layered drink, served in a shot glass. Its success depends on the knowledge and skill of the bartender. Each ingredient is carefully poured into the glass, either down a bar spoon, with the flat end in contact with the surface of the previous ingredient, letting it flow slowly over the top, or over a spoon in contact with the side of the glass and the surface of the drink. Ingredients must be layered according to their alcoholic density. Generally, the higher the density, the lighter the liquid and the more likely it is to float. Start with the non-alcoholic ingredients—such as syrups, which are heavy and will stay at the bottom—then work up to the strongest, lightest liquids. The exception is cream and cream liqueurs, which will rise naturally to the top (like the cream on the top of unhomogenized milk). Like any skill, layering takes practice … but therein lies the fun!

Flaming Drinks

Care must to be taken when igniting drinks. Make sure that there is plenty of space around the glass and that you don't knock it over accidentally. Never carry a drink that is alight. Extinguish the flames by covering the glass gently with a metal tray. Warn the drinker that the rim will be hot, and let it sit awhile so that lips are not burned!

In order to light a drink, the top layer should be a spirit containing at least 40% alcohol.

Shake it baby!

Shaking a drink with cracked or cubed ice will both chill and dilute it. Surprisingly, the more ice you use, the less the drink will be diluted. (Using too little ice will dilute a drink faster than using more since the smaller quantity melts more rapidly.) For best results, fill the cocktail shaker two-thirds full with fresh ice, then add the fruit juices, eggs, or cream, and finally the liquor. Attach the top and cap firmly and, holding the shaker in front of you with one hand firmly clasping the top and the other hand supporting the base, shake the cocktail using a brisk pumping action. Practice this before doing it in front of people as it could be a disaster if your hands slip and the cocktail shaker falls apart all over your guests! After shaking for about fifteen seconds, remove the cap and keep holding the top on while you pour the cocktail through the strainer into the glass. Never shake fizzy ingredients.

Stir it up

Stirring is best done in a lipped mixing glass, in the glass half of a Boston shaker, or in a pitcher with a capacity of at least 1 pint US (16fl oz US/ 500ml). Place cracked or cubed ice in the glass, add the ingredients, then stir the drink with a bar spoon, sliding the back of the spoon down the inside of the mixing glass and twirling it gently between thumb and forefinger.

When stirring drinks with soda or other fizzy liquids the drink will hold its effervescence longer if stirred gently for just a brief time—but don't be too energetic in the stirring! When the glass starts to show condensation on the outside, the drink is chilled and ready for pouring. Use a Hawthorne strainer when pouring the drink into a glass.

Only drinks with clear ingredients should be stirred, the rest should be shaken.

Frosting rims

For added effect, decorate the top of the glass with salt, sugar, chocolate, or even desiccated coconut. The salt frosting on the rim of a margarita glass is achieved by taking a wedge of lime or lemon and running it around the rim of the glass while holding the glass upside down to prevent juice going into the glass or down the stem. Next, dip the glass rim gently into a saucer of salt until evenly coated. For sugary frostings, dip the rim of the glass into the whipped white of an egg or a wet sponge, then into a saucer of sugar. Repeat the procedure a couple of times for an even coating. For even greater effect, match the sugar color to the flavor or color of the drink by mixing it with a few drops of vegetable dye or a colored syrup—such as grenadine. Sugar frosting should only be used for sweetened cocktails.

Chilling Glasses

It's vital that a cocktail is served cold. Glasses can be chilled in the fridge, if you have room, or more rapidly in the freezer. If possible, keep the cocktail shaker chilled too. Alternatively, fill the cocktail glass with ice before use. (Cracked or crushed ice is better for quicker, more even chilling.) It may take a few minutes for the condensation to appear on the glass to show that it is chilled, but this gives you time to prepare and mix the remainder of the ingredients. When the glass is suitably frosted, discard the chilling ice, and pour in your cocktail.

Nice Ice

Ice is the essential cocktail ingredient. A committed bartender will make ice with bottled mineral or spring water, which tastes purer, and stays clearer when frozen. If you're planning to make lots of cocktails, buy bags of ice from your local supermarket or liquor store. Don't be mean when you are putting ice in a drink, . Two cubes won't do—you must fill the glass to keep the drink really cold. There's safety in numbers—the more ice cubes, the longer they will take to melt and dilute the

drink. Once ice has been used in a cocktail shaker or for chilling glasses, discard it and use fresh for the next drink.

Ice can be crushed by hitting the bag of ice, wrapped in dish towel, with a rolling pin. Alternatively, use an electric ice crusher, or a blender that can take the strain. Crack using an ice pick.

Infusions

Any spirit with an alcohol content of 40% or more can be flavored with fruit or spices to give an extra dimension to your cocktails—but it can't be done in a hurry. One exception is chili-flavored vodka. Just add a few slices of fresh chili to the cocktail shaker with the vodka and it will impart the "heat" in a few shakes!

Vodka an ideal base to infuse because it has little flavor of its own. Try it with fruits such as lemon, raspberries, redcurrants, or cranberries. Add sugar to the spirits along with the fruit or lemon parings to make it sweeter and help release the flavors. Macerate for between two and six weeks, depending on the fruit, and shake daily to help dissolve the sugar. Sloes or damsons, in gin, are best left for twelve weeks. Strawberries and cherries are great in brandy, and split vanilla pods added to a bottle of rum add a sweetness that is wonderful in daiquiris. Herbs such as rosemary, bay leaves, or thyme, and spices such as cinnamon, or lemongrass, can also be used to flavor vodka, gin, or whiskey.

Garnishes

Citrus Twists and spirals

When a recipe calls for a "twist" of orange or lemon, a little of the oil from the zest of the fruit should be added to the cocktail along with the citrus. To make a twist, take a piece of fresh fruit and cut a small oval piece of peel with no pith on it. Holding it over the edge of the glass, twist the peel between the thumb and forefinger. This action releases a fine spray of citrus oil onto the surface of the drink—a truly professional touch! Finally, drop the sliver of fruit into the drink.

Use a canelle knife to make citrus peel spirals. Hold the knife against the top of the fruit and steadily drag it round the fruit to get a spiral of peel. Wrap the spiral around a pencil and secure it with a pin, then freeze it for five minutes and the spiral will keep its shape longer in the drink, or when hanging over the side of the glass—as in a "Horse's Neck" cocktail garnish.

Cutting fruit wheels, wedges, and slices

Fruit is ideal for decorating cocktails. You can spear it on a cocktail stick and balance it on the top of the glass, or arrange it carefully on the rim.

Citrus fruits are the easiest to use, though there are many alternatives. A citrus "wheel" is a whole slice of lemon, lime, or orange. Slices can be twisted or "butterflied" to sit on the glass rim. Alternatively, cut citrus fruits into wedges by topping and tailing the fruit, cutting it in half lengthways, then cutting each half into four chunky wedges.

The gamut of garnishes

Some cocktail "pros" shun the use of paper parasols and plastic trinkets for garnishing cocktails, insisting that garnishes should be edible. However, cocktails should be fun, so it's up to you to let your imagination run riot if you want to!

Keep garnishing simple with a single pearl onion on a stick for a Gibson, a single green olive for a Dry Martini, a maraschino cherry (available in red, green, yellow, or blue, with or without stalk) a single grape or a trio, or a stem of redcurrants. Lemons, limes, and oranges are standard, but for a really elaborate cocktail, use wedges of pineapple or pieces of banana or banana leaf.

A natural stirrer can be easily fashioned from a bamboo sprig, a stem of lemon grass, a celery stick, or a length of cucumber. Slivers of chili and slices of cucumber give a savory tang to a drink.

Cinnamon sticks are ideal for use in hot toddies. Peeled or grated chocolate, ground cinnamon, freshly grated nutmeg, or coffee beans are perfect for sprinkling on creamy cocktails.

Fresh borage, lemon balm, or mint will make refreshing and fragrant additions to a Pimms or a Julep. Fresh rose petals or other edible flowers are perfect delicate garnishes. Mango, watermelon, peach, starfruit, kiwi, apple, raspberries, and strawberries look great if really fresh but, like banana, go brown and become tired looking quite quickly.

Decorate with fun swizzle sticks in glass or plastic, straws—small or long, straight, bendy or twisted, plain or stripey—paper parasols or plastic animals and place on smart coasters to really set off the cocktail.

Decorated Ice Cubes

Fill ice cube trays with water and add a leaf or flower—try lemon balm, basil, mint, lemon verbena, sweet geranium leaves, borage flowers, violas, or pansies. Alternatively, add raspberries, cranberries, redcurrants, black currants, or small segments of lemon, lime, or orange. Star anise or pomegranate seeds look very striking, as do slivers of chili or edible gold leaf.

Weights and Measurements

The recipes in this book are based on the measurements for one drink. However ingredients are given in ratio form to make it easy to mix a greater number of cocktails. For one drink, one "part" corresponds to 1 fl oz US or 30ml. You can use whatever type of measure you like; a pony holds 1 fl oz US, a jigger 1 1/2 fl oz US.

	US Imperial	Metric
dash	1/16 fl oz	2ml
bar spoon	1/2 fl oz	15ml
1 tsp	1/6 fl oz	5ml
1 tbsp (3 tsp)	1/2 fl oz	15ml
2 tbsp (pony)	1 fl oz	30ml
3 tbsp (jigger)	1 1/2 fl oz	45ml
1/4 cup	2 fl oz	60ml
1/3 cup	2.5 fl oz	80ml
1/2 cup	4 fl oz	125ml
2/3 cup	5 fl oz	160ml
3/4 cup	6 fl oz	180ml
1 cup	8 fl oz	250ml
1 pint	16 fl oz	500ml

Bellini

Invented in the '40s at Harry's Bar in Venice, the fragrant Bellini cocktail caught on with Americans in the '50s.

3 parts chilled dry champagne
1 part chilled peach juice

Pour the champagne and peach juice into a chilled champagne saucer glass. Stir lightly with a glass swizzle stick. Garnish with a thin slice of peach.

ENTERTAINING?

serve

MOËT

the great Champagne of France

CELEBRATING?

serve

MOËT

the great Champagne of France

Schieffelin & Co., New York

Stinger

Use white crème de menthe for the authentic '50s version of this cocktail.

2 parts brandy
2 parts white crème de menthe
1 part freshly squeezed lime juice

Shake ingredients vigorously in a cocktail shaker with cracked ice. Strain into a chilled highball glass and serve straight up with a twist of lime.

Dry Martini

No other cocktail arouses so much controversy. The ratio of gin to vermouth varies wildly. Here is the classic '50s version.

4 parts gin
1 part dry vermouth

Stir ingredients with cracked ice in a mixing glass. Strain into a chilled cocktail glass and serve straight up. Garnish with a pitted green olive.

21

Sea Mist

A variation on the Sea Breeze, one of the cocktails that became popular in New York in the mid '90s.

3 parts cranberry and raspberry juice
3 parts pink grapefruit juice
2 parts vodka
Slices of lime and lemon frozen in ice cubes

Shake the fruit juices and vodka thoroughly in a cocktail shaker with cracked ice. Strain into a highball glass filled with decorated ice cubes.

Double Vision

A great-tasting, refreshing vodka cocktail.

1 part citron vodka
1 part blackcurrant vodka
1 part apple juice
1 part freshly squeezed lime
  juice
½ part sugar syrup
3 dashes of Angostura bitters

Combine all the ingredients in a cocktail shaker with cracked ice. Shake well, and strain into a cocktail glass. Serve straight up, garnished with a thin slice of apple.

LOBBY CARD FOR THE 1930 FILM *THE BLUE ANGEL*
(DER BLAUE ENGEL) STARRING MARLENE DIETRICH
AND DIRECTED BY JOSEF VON STERNBERG.

Blue Angel

A heavenly drink with delicate floral and violet undertones. Parfait d'amour ("perfect love") is a violet liqueur whose subtle aromas and flavors are obtained from curaçao, orange peel, vanilla pods, almonds, and rose petals.

1 part blue curaçao
1 part Parfait d'amour
1 part brandy
1 part freshly squeezed
  lemon juice
1 part light cream

Shake all the ingredients in a cocktail shaker with cracked ice. Strain into a margarita or cocktail glass. Garnish with a slice of star fruit.

Thai Tiger

A crisp, clean cocktail combining a mixture of sweet and sour flavors synonymous with Thailand. It may look like lemonade but it's got a kick like a Thai boxer! Chili vodka may be used, but adding the fresh chili to plain vodka and shaking it well allows plenty of time for the heat and flavor to come through.

Make lemon-grass and ginger syrup by adding 1 stick of crushed lemongrass, a 1 inch/2.5cm piece of peeled fresh ginger root cut into slivers, and one or two lime leaves to the pan while making ½ pint US/250ml of sugar syrup (see page 12).

1 part lemongrass and ginger syrup (see recipe)
2 parts fresh coconut juice (optional)
1 part vodka
1 small chili, de-seeded and sliced
1½ parts freshly squeezed lime juice
Sprite or 7-up

Combine the flavored syrup, coconut juice (if using), vodka, sliced chili, and lime juice in a cocktail shaker with cracked ice. Shake well. Strain into a highball glass half-filled with crushed ice. Top up with Sprite or 7-up. Garnish with a stick of lemongrass, a sliver of chili, and a slender wedge of lime.

Mai Tai

Created by Victor "Trader Vic" Bergeron, famous for his rum-based cocktails. He made this drink in his San Francisco bar one night in 1944, and asked two friends from Tahiti to try it. "Mai tai ... roa ae!" said one of them, which translates as "Out of this world ... the best!"

1 part light rum
½ part dark rum
1 part orange juice
1 part apricot brandy
½ part tequila
½ part Cointreau or
   triple sec
2 dashes of grenadine
Dash of Amaretto or orgeat
Dash of Angostura bitters

Shake ingredients vigorously in a cocktail shaker with cracked ice. Strain into an old-fashioned glass or large goblet, half-filled with crushed ice. Decorate with slices of orange, lemon, and lime, a maraschino cherry, and a sprig of mint.

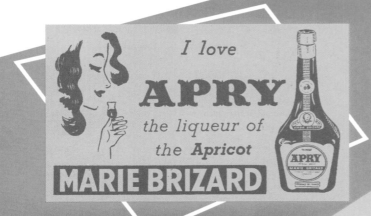

Margarita

The Margarita's origins, like those of all classic cocktails, are shrouded in legend. Its native home, like that of the spirit tequila, is believed to be Mexico. Tales tell of a beautiful woman named Margarita, thwarted love, and a bartender who created a drink in her memory.

2 parts tequila
1 part Cointreau or triple sec
½ part freshly squeezed lime juice

Rub round the rim of a chilled cocktail or margarita glass with a wedge of lime, then dip into fine salt. Shake the ingredients vigorously in a cocktail shaker with cracked ice. Strain into the glass. Serve straight up garnished with a wedge of lime.

Tequila Sunrise

The Tequila Sunrise may have originated at the Agua Caliente racetrack in Mexico in Prohibition times, when Californians drove across the border to take part in the races and enjoy legal hits of liquor. After a long night of imbibing, a pick-me-up of tequila and nutritious orange juice seemed just the thing!

2 parts tequila
5 parts orange juice
½ part grenadine

Pour the tequila and orange juice into a highball glass filled with ice. Stir. When it settles, pour the grenadine in a circle around the top of the drink and let it fall to the bottom. Garnish with a slice of orange and a maraschino cherry.

Moscow Mule

Relations between the United States and Russia were strained in the '50s, as the name of this cocktail suggests! Kitschy mule accessories lend a touch of fun to this fantastic drink.

1½ parts vodka
1 teaspoon freshly squeezed lime juice
Ginger ale

Pour the vodka and the lime juice into a chilled highball glass one-third filled with ice cubes. Fill the glass to the brim with ginger ale. Garnish with a slice of lime.

Red October

A drink for cherry brandy lovers that, after a few, could silently take you out!

1 part vodka
2 parts cherry brandy
7-up

Shake the vodka and cherry brandy in a cocktail shaker with cracked ice. Strain into an old-fashioned glass, half-filled with ice. Top up with a little 7-up. Garnish with maraschino cherries.

Cherry Liqueur
frappé

Passionate Peach Fizz

Really fruity and a touch more exciting than that old favorite, the Bucks Fizz.

2 parts orange juice
2 parts passion fruit juice
½ part peach schnapps
Champagne or sparkling wine

Shake the fruit juices and the peach schnapps vigorously in a cocktail shaker with cracked ice. Strain into a champagne flute and top up with champagne or sparkling wine. Serve straight up with a thin wedge of peach.

"OF ALL THE GIN JOINTS IN ALL THE TOWNS IN THE WORLD, SHE WALKS INTO MINE."
RICK BLAINE (HUMPHREY BOGART) AND ILSA LUND (INGRID BERGMAN) SWAP SMOLDERING LOOKS OVER CHAMPAGNE COCKTAILS IN THE HIT FILM *CASABLANCA* (WARNER BROS.,1942), DIRECTED BY MICHAEL CURTIZ.

Bring your Old Fashioneds up to date

Your first sip of Old Taylor will show you how flavorful
Old Fashioneds can be!

100 proof, bottled in bond Old Taylor is Kentucky bourbon
at its best—*extra*-rich and satisfying.

Prefer milder 86 proof? Ah, then try Old Taylor 86.
Here, Sir, is the lightest *full-flavored* bourbon you can buy!
Each is the finest of its kind.

OLD TAYLOR

"The Noblest Bourbon of Them All"

Straight from
KENTUCKY
a truly American whiskey

Old-fashioned

This simple, venerable whiskey cocktail has always been a popular favorite. Bring it up to date with some wacky accessories and garnishes!

½ teaspoon sugar
2 dashes of Angostura bitters
1 teaspoon water
1½ parts rye

Put the sugar in an old-fashioned glass. Add the bitters and water. Muddle to dissolve the sugar. Add the rye with an ice cube and stir with a glass rod. Garnish with a slice of orange, a slice of pineapple, and a maraschino cherry.

Piña Colada

Translating from the Spanish as "strained pineapple," the Piña Colada started life in the Caribbean and combines many of the island's natural wonders: pineapple, coconut, and, of course, rum! The all-time favorite summer beach cocktail, this is a gorgeous, creamy, fruit creation.

2 parts golden, white, or dark rum
3 parts pineapple juice or ½ cup diced pineapple pieces
1 part coconut cream or fresh coconut milk
½ part light cream
2 dashes of Angostura bitters (optional)

Combine all ingredients with four or five ice cubes in a blender. Blend until smooth. Pour into a large goblet or Boston glass. Garnish with a large wedge of pineapple and a maraschino cherry.

PPIEST DRINK YOU'LL EVER FIND IS EASY-TO-SERVE

Pineapple Juice

NATURE'S MOST REFRESHING FLAVOR

CANNED TROPIC-FRESH

Playtimes or mealtimes—whenever folks are thirsty—glasses of golden Pineapple Juice never fail to "hit the spot". Keep several cans chilling in your refrigerator so it's always ready to serve. And shake each can well before pouring so you enjoy *all* the glorious taste. In this wonderful juice, as in canned Pineapple fruit cuts, Nature stores her most *refreshing* flavor!

SLICES
of canned Pineapple make inviting fruit servings....glamorize salads, main-course meat dishes, bakings....taste wonderful broiled!

CRUSHED
canned Pineapple, good to eat "as is", also helps you make delicious pies, cookies, puddings, icings, sundaes and sauces

CHUNKS
of canned Pineapple—bite size—are fine for fruit cups, to sauté with lamb chops or a roast, for hors d'oeuvres, as cake decoration (Pineapple TIDBITS are smaller)

PINEAPPLE GROWERS ASSOCIATION · SAN FRANCISCO

Millionaire

Sophistication in a glass—take a sip, close your eyes, and wish ...

3 parts bourbon
1 part curaçao
1 egg white
½ part grenadine

Stir ingredients well in a mixing glass with cracked ice. Strain into a chilled cocktail glass and serve straight up. Garnish with a slice of orange.

Glitterati

Opulent and luxurious, this variation on the classic martini has the Midas touch!

2 parts vodka
Dash of dry vermouth
A shred of edible gold leaf

Combine the vodka, vermouth, and gold leaf in a mixing glass. Muddle it with some very finely crushed ice to break up the gold leaf. Pour into a cocktail glass and serve straight up. Garnish with a cocktail onion and two black olives.

Edible gold leaf is available from good delicatessens and specialist food and drink stores.

White Lady

This shimmering, pure white cocktail is full of vintage Hollywood glamor. Imagine Marilyn Monroe sipping one of these wearing *that* white dress.

2 parts gin
1 part Cointreau or triple sec
1 part freshly squeezed lemon juice

Shake ingredients thoroughly with in a cocktail shaker with cracked ice. Strain into a chilled cocktail glass and serve straight up.

CELEBRATED AMERICAN ACTORS MARILYN
MONROE AND DONALD O'CONNOR
(RIGHT) CHAT OVER COCKTAILS WITH
AMERICAN COMPOSER AND LYRICIST
COLE PORTER AT A CINERAMA PARTY
AT THE COCOANUT GROVE, LOS
ANGELES, 1953.

Havana Beach

Sweet and light, this is one of the easiest rum cocktails to make on a summer's day. For ultimate refreshment, chop half a lime into four wedges and add to the cocktail shaker to give the drink a slightly sour lime flavor.

2 parts golden or white Cuban
  rum
3 parts pineapple juice
1 teaspoon sugar syrup
Ginger ale

Shake the rum, pineapple juice, and syrup vigorously in a cocktail shaker with cracked ice. Strain into an old-fashioned glass, half-filled with ice cubes. Top up with ginger ale. Garnish with a few pineapple cubes.

Cuban Peach

You just can't beat the combination of rum and brandy for giving you that relaxing feeling. Lie back and enjoy!

1 part peach brandy
1 part white Cuban rum
1 teaspoon freshly squeezed lime juice
Pinch of sugar

Shake all ingredients thoroughly in a cocktail shaker with cracked ice. Strain into a cocktail glass half-filled with crushed ice. Float two thin slices of peach and a sprig of mint on the top to garnish.

Banana Daiquiri

A variation on the classic American Daiquiri (see page 60), this tropical delight is the perfect vacation drink—an ideal prequel to a lazy afternoon siesta!

1 small banana, peeled and
  sliced
1 part white rum
1 part golden rum
½ part crème de banane
½ part freshly squeezed lime
  juice
½ part coconut milk
1 teaspoon sugar syrup

Blend all ingredients with crushed ice until smooth. Pour into a large, chilled Boston glass. Add a few ice cubes. Garnish with a large twist of banana leaf.

Banana leaves are available from good supermarkets.

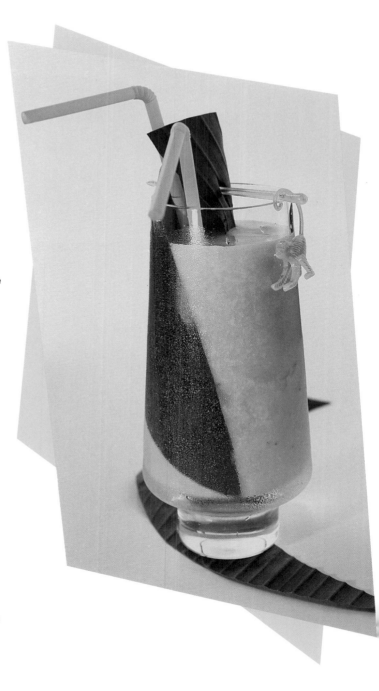

Havana Cocktail

Dark and mysterious, this is a heady mixture, so sip it slowly.

1 part cream sherry
1 part golden rum
1 teaspoon freshly squeezed lemon or lime juice

Shake the ingredients thoroughly in a cocktail shaker with cracked ice. Strain into a cocktail glass. Garnish with a lemon or lime peel twist.

Cosmopolitan

Also known as the "Stealth Martini," this sophisticated pink cocktail has a hidden kick. Drink historians trace its origins back to the gay community in Provincetown, Massachusetts. Popularized during the '80s as a yuppie status symbol, and more recently by *Sex And The City*'s Sarah Jessica Parker, this is a particular favorite of the affluent, young city dweller.

1½ parts citron vodka
1 part Cointreau or triple sec
1 part cranberry juice
Dash of orange bitters
Dash of freshly squeezed lime juice

Shake all ingredients thoroughly in a cocktail shaker with cracked ice. Strain into a chilled cocktail glass. Garnish with pared orange peel and serve straight up.

Limoncello Italiano

An adult version of lemonade! Make your own citron vodka by steeping pared rind from 6 lemons with 4oz US/125g sugar in 24fl oz US/750ml vodka, in a large jar. Shake the jar daily for 3–4 weeks. Once flavoring is complete, strain the vodka back into the vodka bottle. Serve citron vodka as in this recipe, or keep the bottle in the freezer and serve it neat in iced shot glasses.

2 parts vodka or citron vodka (see recipe)
½ part lemon juice
½ part sugar syrup
7-up

Shake the vodka, lemon juice, and syrup in a cocktail shaker with cracked ice. Strain into a highball glass half-filled with crushed ice and a long curled length of lemon peel. Top up with 7-up.

Classic Cocktail

Not to be confused with a Classic Champagne Cocktail (see page 52). A cool, sophisticated drink that will make you feel one in a million!

1½ parts brandy
½ part curaçao
½ part maraschino
½ part freshly squeezed lime juice
½ part sugar syrup

Shake ingredients in a cocktail shaker with cracked ice. Strain into a cocktail glass. Serve straight up and garnish with maraschino cherries.

TWO YOUNG WOMEN CHAT OVER DRINKS
IN A COCKTAIL BAR (1945).

Coq Rouge

This '50s favorite seems to have fallen out of fashion recently. Time for a revival!

2 parts light rum
1 part gin
1 part freshly squeezed lemon or lime juice
1 part Cointreau or triple sec

Stir or shake with cracked ice. Strain into a chilled cocktail glass and serve straight up. Garnish with a twist of orange peel.

Frisco

"San Francisco! It is and has everything," said poet Dylan Thomas in 1952—including this exquisite cocktail, of course.

2 parts rye
1 part Benedictine
½ part freshly squeezed lemon juice

Shake ingredients thoroughly in a cocktail shaker with cracked ice. Strain into a chilled cocktail glass and serve straight up. Garnish with a twist of lemon peel.

Long Island Iced Tea

This popular cocktail dates back to Prohibition times, so don't be fooled by its innocuous name and pale brown color! A cool, refreshing happy hour favorite, great for sipping on the veranda on a balmy summer evening.

½ part golden rum
½ part gin
½ part vodka
½ part tequila
½ part Cointreau or triple sec
½ part sugar syrup
1 part freshly squeezed lime juice
Cola

Combine all ingredients, except the cola, in a cocktail shaker with cracked ice. Shake well. Strain into a highball glass half-filled with ice. Top up with a dash of cola and garnish with a wedge of lime.

Classic Champagne Cocktail

The epitome of sophistication, the Classic Champagne Cocktail can be served in one of two different glasses: in the flute, as pictured, or in a saucer-shaped champagne glass.

1 cube of sugar
1 teaspoon brandy
3 dashes of Angostura bitters
Chilled dry champagne

Put the cube of sugar into a chilled champagne glass. Sprinkle with the brandy and Angostura bitters. Pour the champagne into the glass and stir lightly with a glass swizzle stick to mix. Garnish with a twist of lemon peel.

ACTORS HUMPHREY BOGART AND AUDREY HEPBURN
FLIRT OVER A CHAMPAGNE COCKTAIL IN *SABRINA FAIR*
(PARAMOUNT, 1954) DIRECTED BY BILLY WILDER.

Planters' Punch

This long, summer drink was first developed on southern plantations of the United States in the mid-nineteenth century. Its popularity has endured to the present day.

3 parts dark Jamaican rum
1 part freshly squeezed lime juice
1 teaspoon sugar
Dash of Angostura bitters
Club soda

Shake the rum, lime juice, sugar, and bitters in a cocktail shaker with cracked ice. Strain into a highball glass half-filled with crushed ice. Add club soda to fill. Garnish with a maraschino cherry, a cube of pineapple, a slice of orange, and a sprig of mint.

RusTY Nail

The Drambuie sweetens and softens the whiskey with its subtle heather tones. Refreshingly simple, and a great favorite with Scotch drinkers.

2 parts Scotch
1 part Drambuie

Combine ingredients with ice in a mixing glass and stir. Strain into an old-fashioned glass filled with ice. Garnish with a long twist of lemon rind.

Whiskey Sour

Sour by name, sour by nature, this traditional gentleman's drink should be served plain and simple in an old-fashioned glass.

2 parts rye
1 part freshly squeezed lemon juice
1 teaspoon sugar

Shake vigorously in a cocktail shaker with cracked ice, until foamy. Pour into a chilled old-fashioned glass. Garnish with a twist of lemon peel.

Whiskey Sour, anyone?

OLD TAYLOR
"The Noblest Bourbon of Them All"

Kiwi Kraze

This terrific cocktail is especially tasty when made with fresh kiwi fruit, although using the ready-made juice is quicker and less time-consuming.

3 parts kiwi fruit juice
1 part gin
Dash of absinthe
Tonic water

Shake the kiwi juice, gin and a good dash of absinthe in a cocktail shaker with cracked ice. Strain into an old-fashioned glass half-filled with crushed ice. Top up with tonic water. Garnish with a slice of kiwi fruit.

Caribbean Champagne Cocktail

Looks and tastes delightfully decadent!

¼ part light rum
¼ part crème de banane
Dash of Angostura bitters
Chilled champagne

Pour the rum, crème de banane, and Angostura bitters into a champagne flute. Top with champagne and stir gently with a glass rod. Decorate with slices of banana, a maraschino cherry, and a pineapple leaf.

Daiquiri

An American classic, the daiquiri originates from the iron mines in the Cuban town of Daiquiri around the turn of the century when American mining engineers drank a mixture of the local rum, lime juice, and sugar to ward off tropical fevers.

3 parts light rum
1 part freshly squeezed lime
  juice
1/2 teaspoon sugar syrup

Shake in a cocktail shaker with cracked ice. Strain into a chilled cocktail glass and serve straight up. Garnish with a slice of lime and a maraschino cherry.

Red

Wherever people of discrimination meet - CINZANO VERMOUTH is the drink they choose. RED or BIANCO (white).... 'straight' or 'on the rocks'.... to enjoy the full, delicious flavour of these unique Vermouths.*

CINZANO

VERMOUTH

FRANCESCO CINZANO

TORINO

VERMOUTH

A TEACHER AT A BARTENDING SCHOOL DEMONSTRATES THE PROCEDURES FOR MIXING ALCOHOLIC DRINKS TO A CLASS OF MALE STUDENTS (CIRCA 1945).

Sloe Gin Fizz

Combined deliciously with sweet vermouth and club soda, sloe gin liquor becomes sparkling heaven in a glass!

3 parts sloe gin
2 parts sweet vermouth
1 part freshly squeezed lemon juice
Club soda

Shake the gin, vermouth, and lemon juice vigorously in a cocktail shaker with cracked ice. Strain into a highball glass. Add ice cubes and fill the glass with club soda.

Lemon Meringue Martini

Created in London in the year 2000, this cocktail tastes even better than lemon meringue pie! Smooth and creamy with a sharp lemon twang— and none of that soggy pastry!

2 parts citron vodka
1 part Drambuie
1 part freshly squeezed lemon juice
1–2 teaspoons sugar syrup

Shake all ingredients thoroughly with cracked ice in a cocktail shaker. Strain into a cocktail glass. Garnish with a lemon peel twist.

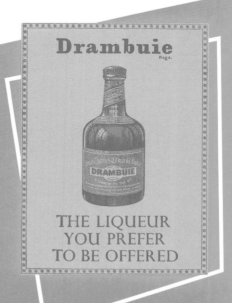

Drambuie Regd.

DRAMBUIE

THE LIQUEUR
YOU PREFER
TO BE OFFERED

Saketini

Though often referred to as "rice wine," sake is, in fact, a rice beer. It is traditionally served warm in small cups in Japanese restaurants but can also be served at room temperature or even chilled. The subtle orangey notes of the sake make the Saketini a mouth-watering appetizer cocktail.

2 parts sake
1 part vodka
½ part gin
½ part Cointreau or triple sec

Combine the ingredients with cracked ice in a mixing glass. Stir and strain into a cocktail glass. Serve straight up and garnish with a slice of cucumber and sliver of scallion.

Pink Lady

The addition of grenadine makes this drink a pretty Barbie-doll pink. Don't be fooled by appearances though—it's more potent than it looks!

2 parts applejack
2 parts gin
1 part freshly squeezed lime
    juice
1 part grenadine
1 egg white

Frost the rim of a chilled cocktail glass with grenadine syrup and sugar (see page 14). Shake all the ingredients in a cocktail shaker with cracked ice. Strain into the cocktail glass and serve straight up. Garnish with a maraschino cherry.

Applejack

The early American settlers distilled hard cider to make applejack and drank it neat. By the '50s, however, tastes had become a little more refined.

1 part applejack
1 part grapefruit juice
Dash of grenadine

Stir or shake the ingredients with cracked ice. Strain into a cocktail glass filled with crushed ice and serve with a twist of lemon.

Alexander

**This creamy delight is more commonly
made with brandy, but the gin
alternative shown here was popular in
the United States in the '50s.**

2 parts gin
1 part crème de cacao
1 part heavy cream

Shake ingredients vigorously in a cocktail shaker
with cracked ice. Strain into a chilled cocktail glass
and serve straight up. For the finishing touch,
sprinkle with a fine dusting of cocoa.

I. W. HARPER
. . . it's always
a pleasure
GENUINE ORIGINAL I. W. HARPER
IS AVAILABLE AT
100 PROOF • BOTTLED IN BOND
and
MILDER 86 PROOF
DISTILLERY BOTTLED
I. W. HARPER
since 1872
The Gold Medal Whiskey
KENTUCKY STRAIGHT BOURBON

Mint Julep

The first Saturday in May—the running of the Kentucky Derby—is the traditional start of the Mint Julep season.

1 teaspoon sugar
1 tablespoon chopped mint leaves
1 tablespoon water
1½ parts bourbon
1 small bunch of fresh mint

Put the sugar and chopped mint in a mortar and bruise the leaves with a pestle to make a paste. Add the water and continue stirring. Fill an old-fashioned glass half-full with crushed ice. Add the mint syrup and bourbon. Fill the glass with more crushed ice and tuck the bunch of mint into the ice with a couple of short straws.

Moulin Rouge

Full of fun, fruitiness, and fizz—a few of these and you'll start singing and doing the high kicks without a stage!

4 parts pineapple juice
½ part brandy
Champagne or sparkling wine

Shake the pineapple juice and brandy thoroughly in a cocktail shaker with cracked ice. Strain into a highball glass, half-filled with crushed ice. Top up with champagne or sparkling wine and stir.

FOUR CHICAGO GIRLS PERFORM EXERCISES FOR MAKING COCKTAILS IN PREPARATION FOR THE NATIONAL LIQUOR CONVENTION, OPENING AT THE STEVENS HOTEL, CHICAGO, ON MARCH 11TH, 1935, IN WHICH THEY WILL TAKE PART.

Orange Blossom

1 part gin
1 part orange juice

Considered a ladies' drink back in the '50s, this refreshing mixture of pure orange juice and gin is now a treat for everyone.

Shake ingredients vigorously in a cocktail shaker with cracked ice. Strain into a chilled old-fashioned glass and serve straight up. Garnish with a slice of orange.

Tom Collins

Sweet, sugary, and sophisticated, this drink lends its name to the Collins glass, an essential piece of glassware for any serious bartender!

2 parts gin
1 part freshly squeezed lemon juice
1 part sugar syrup
Club soda

Shake ingredients thoroughly in a cocktail shaker with cracked ice. Strain into a Collins glass. Add ice cubes and fill the glass with club soda. Garnish with mint leaves

Singapore Sling

Created by the barman at Singapore's Raffles Hotel in 1915, the Singapore Sling saw a revival during the '50s due to the fascination with South Seas' umbrella drinks.

2 parts gin
1 part cherry brandy
½ part freshly squeezed lemon juice
Dash of Benedictine
Dash of Cointreau or triple sec
Club soda

Shake the gin, cherry brandy, lemon, Benedictine and Cointreau in a cocktail shaker with cracked ice. Strain into a chilled Collins glass. Add ice cubes and club soda to fill the glass. Garnish with orange and lemon slices and a maraschino cherry.

THE SHORT DRINK THAT GOES A LONG WAY!

De KUYPER *Cherry Brandy*

Made in Holland with finest cherries and genuine brandy

ALSO DE KUYPER HOLLANDS & 'BLACK HEN' ADVOCAAT

THE RAFFLES HOTEL, ONCE DESCRIBED BY SOMERSET MAUGHAM AS THE LEGENDARY SYMBOL FOR "ALL THE FABLES OF THE EXOTIC EAST," IS THE BIRTHPLACE OF THE CELEBRATED SINGAPORE SLING.

Shake it baby!

Clover Club

This fragrant and colorful cocktail is the ideal drink for a summer barbecue party.

2 parts gin
1 part grenadine
1 egg white
1-2 teaspoons freshly
  squeezed lime juice

Shake ingredients in a cocktail shaker with cracked ice. Strain into a chilled cocktail glass and serve straight up with a twist of lime zest.

Harvey Wallbanger

This is a classic Screwdriver, spiked with Galliano, as preferred by Harvey, a Californian surfer in the '70s. Legend has it that, on leaving his local bar one night after several of these, he walked into the wall with his surfboard. He was nicknamed "The Wallbanger," and the rest is history!

4 parts orange juice
2 parts vodka
½ part Galliano

Pour the orange juice and the vodka into a highball glass filled with ice. Stir, and then float the Galliano on the top. Garnish with orange slices.

Mudslide

Also called Muddy Water. The name doesn't really suit the delicate and refreshing creaminess of this iced coffee—but drink one too many and you could start sliding!

1 part vodka
1 part Kahlua or coffee liqueur
1 part Irish cream liqueur

Shake ingredients vigorously in a cocktail shaker with cracked ice. Strain into an old-fashioned glass filled with ice. Garnish with coffee beans.

White Russian

A **Black Russian is straight vodka and coffee liqueur, which is sometimes** served over ice in a highball glass and topped up with cola. This variation is for those who love cocktails with a smooth, velvety texture.

2 parts vodka
1 part Kahlua or coffee liqueur
1–1½ parts light cream

Shake the vodka and Kahlua in a cocktail shaker with cracked ice and strain into an ice-filled old-fashioned glass. Float the cream on top using the back of a bar spoon.

all America welcomes...

VODKA by **GILBEY'S**
the best name vodka ever had

Have you joined your friends in making the most welcome discovery in vodka...smooth, smooth Vodka by Gilbey's? It's made by the world-famous makers of Gilbey's Gin. And Gilbey's uses a costlier distilling process that produces perfectly clarified vodka...clear, true, brilliant in tone...vodka that does best by your drinks and by you.

VODKA 80 & 100 PROOF. DISTILLED FROM 100% GRAIN, W. & A. GILBEY, LTD., CINCINNATI, O. GILBEY'S DISTILLED LONDON DRY GIN, 90 PROOF, 100% GRAIN NEUTRAL SPIRITS. W. & A. GILBEY, LTD., CINCINNATI, O. DISTRIBUTED BY NATIONAL DISTILLERS PRODUCTS CORPORATION.

Sazerac

A quintessential New Orleans drink, claimed by some to be the first cocktail ever created. Invented in the early 19th-century by Antoine Peychaud, a Creole apothecary who moved to New Orleans from the West Indies, the drink was popularized by the Sazerac Coffee House on Exchange Alley. Sazerac was originally made with Sazerac brandy and served in a coquetier. It is now a herbal bourbon classic.

1 part absinthe
Chilled water
1 part bourbon
1 part brandy
½ part sugar syrup
6 drops of Angostura bitters
6 drops of Peychaud's bitters

Fill an old-fashioned glass with ice, pour in the absinthe, fill it up with water, and set aside. Shake the remaining ingredients in a cocktail shaker with cracked ice. Discard the watery absinthe then strain the bourbon mixture into the flavored glass.

Sparkling Bouquet

This spectacular melon flavored cocktail has an aura of psychedelic '60s flower power but with a touch more subtlety of looks and fruity, flowery tones. For added fragrance, add a dash of elderflower syrup to the sparkling wine.

1 part melon liqueur
Sparkling wine

Pour the melon liqueur into a cocktail glass or champagne saucer. Top up with chilled sparkling wine and decorate with fragrant petals and flowers.

Dubonnet Cocktail

Particularly popular in the '50s, Dubonnet rouge is a French aperitif made from red wine flavored with quinine and bitter herbs. If you prefer a drier cocktail, just add more gin.

1 part gin
1 part Dubonnet rouge

Shake ingredients vigorously in a cocktail shaker with cracked ice. Serve either straight up or on the rocks in an old-fashioned glass. Garnish with a twist of lemon peel.

White Wine Cooler

Refreshing (though a little on the sharp side!) and fairly innocuous, unless you add a dash of brandy. Add a dash of Angostura bitters and a dash of kummel (colorless caraway liqueur) or a little sugar, if desired.

4 parts dry white wine
½ part freshly squeezed lemon juice
½ part orange juice
½ part brandy (optional)
Club soda

Pour the wine and fruit juices, and brandy (if using) into an ice-filled highball glass. Top up with club soda and stir gently with a glass rod. Garnish with two thin slices of cucumber.

English Rose

The cool, refreshing color and flavor of the English Rose make it an unusual drink. Its classic '20s style inspires elegance and sophistication.

3 parts extra dry vermouth
1½ parts kirsch
1 part Parfait d'amour

Combine the ingredients in a mixing glass with cracked ice. Stir well. Strain into a cocktail glass. Decorate by floating a rose petal or two on top.

Polish Vodka Scoop

This cocktail may look like a kid's ice cream, but the grassy flavor of the Polish vodka is just enough of a giveaway. Use plain vodka if you want to deceive! Reduce the sweetness by using club soda or tonic water instead of 7-up to top up.

2–3 small scoops lemon ice cream
1 part polish vodka
7-up

Put the ice cream scoops into a chilled goblet or short-stemmed glass. Pour the vodka over the top, and top up with 7-up. Garnish with a twist of lemon peel. Serve with a dessert spoon.

Windward Island

Dark, cool, and refreshing—perfect for those who enjoy their cola with an added depth.

1 part golden rum
½ part Tia Maria
Cola

Shake the rum and Tia Maria vigorously in a cocktail shaker with cracked ice. Strain into an old-fashioned glass almost filled with ice cubes. Top up with cola and garnish with orange slices.

Couples enjoying exotic cocktails at a beachside restaurant, Waikiki Beach in Honolulu, Hawaii.

Manhattan

This New York classic has spawned a host of variations over the years. Here is the original '50s version.

2 parts rye
1 part dry vermouth
1 part sweet vermouth
Dash of Angostura bitters

Stir ingredients in a mixing glass with cracked ice. Strain into a cocktail glass and serve straight up. Garnish with a slice of lemon.

Bronx

Johnnie Solon, the celebrated bartender at the old Waldorf-Astoria in Manhattan, christened this cocktail in honor of the Bronx Zoo.

2 parts gin
2 parts dry vermouth
1 part sweet vermouth
⅓ part orange juice

Shake ingredients vigorously in a cocktail shaker with cracked ice. Strain into a chilled cocktail glass and serve straight up with a twist of orange peel.

Sidecar

This zingy little cocktail is a fantastic winter warmer!

3 parts brandy
1 part Cointreau or triple sec
1 part freshly squeezed lemon juice

Shake ingredients vigorously in a cocktail shaker with cracked ice. Strain into a chilled cocktail glass and serve straight up with a twist of lemon and a maraschino cherry.

Bucks Fizz

Bucks Fizz is many people's first introduction to cocktails. Served at weddings and parties because it's easy to make and ekes out the champagne without looking too mean! Invented in the early '20s to tickle the palate.

2 parts orange juice
Champagne

Pour the orange juice into a champagne flute and top up with champagne.

Basil Vice

A delicious palate cleanser—great between courses, or to spur your taste-buds into action at the start of a meal. Add more vodka if desired.

2 basil leaves
½ part vodka
Dash of raspberry syrup

Roll the basil leaves up tightly, cut into thin strips and chop finely. Place them in the bottom of a shot glass, then almost fill with crushed ice. Pour in the vodka, stir and add a dash of raspberry syrup.

Bloody Mary

Vodka drinks gained popularity in the '50s. This rich red concoction was, then as now, perfect as a pick-me-up or hangover buster.

1 part vodka
2 parts tomato juice
¼ part freshly squeezed lemon juice
1 teaspoon Worcestershire sauce
2 dashes of Tabasco sauce
1 pinch celery salt

Shake ingredients gently in a cocktail shaker with cracked ice to keep the tomato juice from separating. Pour into a chilled highball or Collins glass. Garnish with a celery stalk.

How to Make a
WOW
of a
Cocktail!

Fill glass with ice-cold tomato juice...

Add a pinch of salt and pepper...

Add a teaspoon of **FRENCH'S** Worcestershire Sauce— THAT'S ALL!

New Non-Drip Bottle lets you shake or pour

Buena Vista

"Buena vista" means a good view—the perfect description of this dazzling transparent aqua-blue cocktail. A beautiful drink to sip while you day dream.

1 part white rum
1 part blue curaçao
1 part sugar syrup
1 part freshly squeezed lime juice

Shake all ingredients vigorously in a cocktail shaker with cracked ice. Strain into a highball glass. Garnish with a wedge of lemon.

Meloso! Delicioso!

because it's "Mountain Distilled"

Smooth and delicious! This rum, Senor, is a harmony of taste, blending zestfully into so many delectable drinks. You'll find Ron Merito distinctive, because it is mountain-bred and born in sunny Puerto Rico. There soil, water and tropic air unite with patient human skill to give you rum with a matchless "mountain flavor." Remember — the better the rum, the better the drink. Make your cuba libre, collins, daiquiri or other favorite drink with "mountain distilled" Ron Merito — and make it *delicioso!*

Ron
MERITO

THE PUERTO RICAN MOUNTAIN RUM

SEND FOR FREE COLORFUL 24-PAGE RECIPE BOOKLET

Knickerbocker

Use the syrups from canned raspberries and pineapple to give this drink a tangy sweetness.

5 parts light rum
1 part freshly squeezed lemon
  juice
1 part raspberry syrup
1 part pineapple syrup

Shake ingredients thoroughly in a cocktail shaker with cracked ice. Strain into a chilled cocktail glass and serve straight up. Garnish with twists of orange peel and a maraschino cherry.

Acapulco Gold

A daiquiri by any other name. A smooth, tropical cocktail that's so delicious, you could drink it all day!

2 parts pineapple juice
1 part grapefruit juice
1 part tequila
1 part golden rum
1 part coconut milk

Combine all the ingredients in a cocktail shaker with cracked ice. Shake well. Strain into a Boston glass half-filled with ice cubes. Decorate with a fun straw and a monkey in a palm tree.

Not Tonight Josephine

A mixture that would render even Napoleon harmless!

3 parts red wine
1 part Napoleon brandy
Dash of Pernod

Pour the red wine into a brandy glass with a couple of ice cubes. Add the brandy and Pernod. Stir, and garnish with cocktail onions and a marashino cherry.

Adieux de Napoléon à La Garde Impériale à Fontainebleau. Détail de la peinture par E.J.H.Vernet.

Napoleon bids farewell to his Imperial Guard at Fontainebleau, April 20, 1814, shortly before abdicating. General Petit, Commandant, embraces him.

COURVOISIER

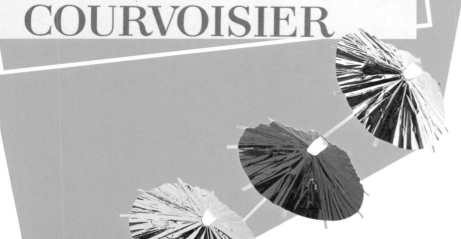

BACARDI of course

Bacardi

Forget Bacardi and Coke! Back in the '50s this delectable ruby-red drink, the classic Bacardi cocktail, was far more popular.

2 parts light Bacardi rum
1 part freshly squeezed lemon or
   lime juice
1 part grenadine

Shake ingredients thoroughly in a cocktail shaker with cracked ice. Strain into a chilled old-fashioned glass and serve straight up. Garnish with a slice of lemon and a maraschino cherry.

Miami

In the 50s, wealthy New Yorkers often wintered in Florida, traveling there in luxurious Pullman trains. This zingy cocktail is a must for the in-car bartenders' repertoire.

5 parts light rum
2 parts freshly squeezed lemon juice
2 parts white crème de menthe

Shake thoroughly in a cocktail shaker with cracked ice. Strain into a chilled cocktail glass and serve straight up. Garnish with a twist of orange peel.

Between the Sheets

This cocktail was created in Harry's New York Bar in Paris in the '30s as a variation on the classic Sidecar (see page 92). The addition of rum makes this cocktail more exciting while beautifully well balanced and refreshing.

1 part light rum
1 part brandy
1 part Cointreau or triple sec
1 part freshly squeezed lemon juice
½ part sugar syrup (optional)

Combine all the ingredients in a cocktail shaker with cracked ice. Shake well. Strain into a chilled cocktail glass. Serve straight up.

JOAN FONTAINE AND HARRY BELAFONTE IN THE 1957 FILM *ISLAND IN THE SUN* (20TH CENTURY FOX) DIRECTED BY ROBERT ROSSEN.

Kir

Created by French farm laborers in Burgundy, who added crème de cassis to their Bourgogne Aligote wine to make it more palatable, and named the result after the colorful war hero and Mayor of Dijon, Canon Felix Kir. A quick and simple drink for a steamy summer's day. The usual ratio is 7 parts white wine to 1 part crème de cassis for a clean, crisp blackcurrant flavor. If you're having a party, substitute champagne for white wine to create a Kir Royale.

½ part crème de cassis
Chilled dry white wine

Pour crème de cassis into a large chilled wine glass or goblet, then top up with white wine and stir gently. Serve straight up.

A_b F_ab

**In reverence to Patsy and Edina from
Absolutely Fabulous this cocktail was
created in London, using their favorites—
"Bolly" and "Stoli".**

1 part Stolichnaya vodka
2 parts cranberry and raspberry juice
Bollinger champagne

Shake the vodka and cranberry juice in a cocktail
shaker with cracked ice and strain into a cocktail
glass. Top up with champagne. Serve straight up.

Raspberry Crush

A really quick way of making raspberry gin.

15 fresh raspberries
1 part gin
1 part framboise or sugar syrup
Dash of freshly squeezed lemon juice
Club soda

Combine the fruit, gin, framboise or sugar syrup and
lemon juice with half a glass of crushed ice in a blender.
Blend until puréed. Pour into an old-fashioned glass, and
add a little club soda to top up the glass. Garnish with
raspberries and mint leaves.

Sherry Flip

A surprisingly pleasant and creamy drink—not just for aged aunts!

1 medium-sized egg
4 parts cream sherry

Shake or blend the egg and sherry with about 6 ice cubes until smooth. Pour into a small goblet. Decorate the top with freshly grated nutmeg.

HARVEY'S

The language of the fan is to-day as much a part of Spanish life as in times gone by. The message here is unusual, but none the less inviting...

HARVEY'S

BRISTOL CREAM
BRISTOL MILK
BRISTOL DRY

TORRE

Butterfield.

Austin Powers

Wacky color and outrageous '60s style, the Austin Powers is an extremely drinkable cocktail—that's if you can bear to be seen with it! Groovy, baby!

3 parts clear apple juice
1 part spiced golden rum
½ part Amaretto
½ part blue curaçao
½ part freshly squeezed
  lime juice

Shake all ingredients thoroughly in a cocktail shaker with cracked ice. Strain into a Boston or highball glass half-filled with ice. Garnish with slices of orange, starfruit, strawberry, and a maraschino cherry. Serve with straws and a parasol.

Zombie

A zombie is a snake god of voodoo cults in West Africa, Haiti, and the Southern United States. According to voodoo belief, the zombie can use its supernatural powers to enter into and reanimate a corpse. This tall, refreshing drink may give you a new lease of life, or, by the end of the evening, render you completely comatose!

1 part dark rum
1 part light rum
1 part golden rum
½ part apricot brandy
½ part curaçao
2 parts orange juice
2 parts pineapple juice
½ part grenadine syrup
1 part freshly squeezed lime juice

Shake all the ingredients vigorously in a cocktail shaker with cracked ice. Strain into an ice-filled Boston glass. Float ½ part overproof rum* on top. Garnish with a long twist of orange.

* Overproof or high strength rum is any rum with over 57% alcohol per volume.

Spanish Sizzler

A fun and bubbly dessert drink. Strangely, the sorbet doesn't dissolve into the Cava so the drink remains clear.

3 small scoops of lemon sorbet
Spanish Cava

Put the sorbet scoops into a chilled goblet. Top up with Cava. Serve with a dessert spoon.

Fireball

This warming combination of classic Scotch and whiskey liqueur has a mighty kick. Watch out—you might get burnt!

1 part Glayva
1 part Glenfiddich

Three-quarters fill a thin-stemmed glass with crushed ice and pour in the Glayva and Glenfiddich together. Stir gently.

David Niven stealing a furtive cocktail in his role as the butler Godfrey in *My Man Godfrey* (Universal, 1957), directed by Henry Koster.

Mexican Wave

1 part tequila
½ part crème de cassis
½ part sugar syrup
Ginger ale

Shake the tequila, crème de cassis, and sugar
syrup in a cocktail shaker with cracked ice.
Strain into an old-fashioned glass, top up with
ginger ale, and mix with a glass swizzle stick.
Float a few thin lime slices on top to garnish.

MEXICO

WARM WEATHER and
a WARM WELCOME
await you in Mexico,
where luxury and
comfort combine with
ancient and colorful
surroundings

ASOCIACION MEXICANA DE HOTELES, MEXICO, D. F.
DEPARTAMENTO HOTELERO

Tijuana Café

A deliciously creamy coffee cocktail.

5fl oz US/160ml hot black coffee
1 part Kahlua or coffee liqueur
1 teaspoon sugar
3 parts heavy cream
1 cinnamon stick

Pour the hot coffee into a warm heatproof coffee glass. Stir in the liqueur and sugar then spoon the lightly whipped cream on top so that it floats. Give it a gentle stir with a cinnamon stick and sprinkle with ground cinnamon.

Almond Breeze

This cocktail looks like an innocent bubbly lime lemonade—but watch out—it has hidden depths!

1 part white rum
½ part Dash of Amaretto or orgeat
½ part melon liqueur
Tonic water

Shake the rum and liqueurs in a cocktail shaker with cracked ice. Strain into a highball glass, half-filled with crushed ice. Top up with tonic water.

Sloe Gin & Tonic

A sweet and sour gin and tonic with the kick and color from sloes. A delicious alternative to Pimms on those endless mid-summer afternoons.

1 part gin
1 part good sloe gin
1 part freshly squeezed lime juice
½ part sugar syrup
Tonic water

Shake the gins, lime juice, and sugar syrup in a cocktail shaker with cracked ice and strain into an ice-filled highball glass. Top up with tonic water and serve with a wedge of lime.

Blue Blazer

A spectacular, combustible treat to be attempted only by experienced bartenders!

1 part Scotch
1 part boiling water
1 teaspoon sugar

Combine the whiskey and the water in a pewter mug or toddy glass. Ignite the liquid and, while it is blazing, carefully pour it back and forth from one mug to another. If done correctly, it will look like a continuous stream of liquid fire. Sweeten with the sugar. Serve with a twist of lemon peel.

Festive Flare

A hot punch best made in large quantities and offered as a warm drink for guests on cold winter evenings.

2 tablespoons brown sugar
2 tablespoons water
2 tablespoons orange juice
Small piece of cinnamon stick
1 star anise
5fl oz US/160ml red wine
1 tablespoon golden or dark rum

Put the sugar, water, orange juice, piece of cinnamon stick and star anise into a small pan and heat gently until the sugar dissolves, then bring almost to the boil. Leave off the heat for 10 minutes to allow the flavors to infuse. Add the wine to the pan and warm it through. Remove the cinnamon stick and pour into a warmed toddy glass. Measure the rum into a small soup ladle, warm the ladle over the gas flame, gently shaking it until hot vapors ignite the rum. Carefully pour the flaming rum into the glass of warm wine. Let the flames die down and the top of the glass cool before you drink it.

Sol y Sombre

The name means sun and shade. Watch out—like the sun, the brandy burns as it goes down!

1 part anisette
1 part brandy

Pour the anisette into a shot glass and carefully add the brandy, over the back of a bar spoon (see page 12) so that it sits on top of the anisette.

Bazooka Joe Shooter

Fabulous colors, fascinating to create.

½ part blue curaçao
½ part crème de banane
½ part Irish cream liqueur

Pour the curaçao into a shot glass, followed by the crème de banane. Float the Irish cream liqueur on top. The yellow crème de banane will sink to the bottom and mix with the curaçao to create a luminous green layer beneath the Irish cream.

A little Hennessy can be a big comfort in the home

HENNESSY
COGNAC BRANDY

IN FLASKS TO SUIT ALL POCKETS

Is there a Hennessy in the House?

Dangerous Detox

A detox shooter with an added layer of danger! Not easy to construct, but if you succeed, you deserve to sample this fantastic combination of flavors.

½ part peach schnapps
½ part cranberry juice
½ part vodka
Dash of absinthe

Carefully pour the ingredients into a shot glass in order of density, as listed in the recipe above, so that you have three equal layers and a thin green line of absinthe at the top.

Electric Flag

You'll need skill and practice to knock this one back all at once!

½ part grenadine syrup
½ part Parfait d'amour
½ part kirsch or grappa

Pour the grenadine syrup into the shot glass. Carefully add the Parfait d'amour, and then the kirsch or grappa, using a bar spoon if required.

Tempting Trio

Three cream liqueur flavors in one glass—delicious!

½ part green crème de menthe
½ part crème de banane
½ part Irish cream liqueur

Carefully layer the crème de menthe, crème de banane, and Irish cream liqueur into a shot glass using the reverse of a bar spoon.

Red Sky at Night

Dash of freshly squeezed lemon juice
7-up
½ part crème de cassis

Fill a chilled highball glass with ice and add a good dash of lemon juice. Pour in 7-up to almost fill the glass, and stir in the crème de cassis.

...ES HAVEN'T HAD ANY FUN FOR 3000 YEARS

...taurant and COCKTAIL LOUNGE "Featuring"
Cocktails... World's Finest Mixed Drinks...

ADVERTISEMENT FOR GIMBEL'S RESTAURANT AND
COCKTAIL LOUNGE, RANDOLPH STREET WEST,
CHICAGO (CIRCA 1940).

Barbie Girl

A little pink coloring and
   sugar, for frosting
5 very large ripe strawberries
1 slice pineapple
1 part orange juice
1 part freshly squeezed lemon
   juice

Frost the top of a large chilled
cocktail glass by dipping it in
coloring then in sugar (see page
14). Combine the fruit and juices in
a blender, with four or five ice
cubes. Blend until smooth. Pour into
the frosted glass and decorate with
slices of strawberry.

Sunshine Sparkle

1 ripe peach
3 parts pineapple juice
2 parts orange juice
½ part freshly squeezed lemon juice
Dash of raspberry syrup
7-up

Cut off a large slice of peach for the garnish. Pit and peel the remainder and combine with the pineapple, orange, and lemon juices and four ice cubes in a blender. Blend until smooth. Pour into a Boston glass half-filled with ice. Add a dash of raspberry syrup and top up with 7-up. Garnish with the slice of peach, a slice of orange, a slice of lemon, and some raspberries on a cocktail stick.

Amber Fizz

4fl oz US/125ml orange juice
Ginger ale

Fill an old-fashioned glass with ice then half fill with orange juice. Top up with ginger ale. Float a piece of pared orange rind on top to garnish.

Pipers, peers, policemen (all the Commonwealth) Cheer for juicy Outspan— Oranges for health!

for Orange

Waiting for something? Spectating —or something? Wherever there's a crowd, people are enjoying everybody's favourite treat—delicious, juicy, thin-skinned, full-of-sunshine Outspan Oranges! And luscious, tangy Outspan Grapefruit for breakfast make even a Monday seem fun-day! Outspan Oranges and Grapefruit are lovely to eat and good for you!

for Outspan

OUTSPAN

You can buy wonderful Outspans wherever you see this sign.

The golden fruit from sunny South Africa

Apple wise

4fl oz US/125ml sparkling
  apple juice
Ginger ale

Half fill a highball glass with ice
cubes. Pour in the apple juice to
three quarters fill the glass. Top
up with ginger ale. Garnish with
a wedge of apple.

Chinese Cheer

1 part freshly squeezed lime juice
1 part freshly squeezed lemon juice
1 teaspoon finely grated fresh ginger root
1½ parts sugar syrup
1 star anise ice cube
Sparkling water

Combine the lime and lemon juices with the ginger and sugar syrup in a cocktail shaker. Shake vigorously with cracked ice. Strain into a chilled old-fashioned glass. Add decorated ice cube and top up with sparkling water.

Bamboozle

3 parts guava juice
2 parts orange juice
2 parts passion fruit juice
Dash of freshly squeezed lime juice
Club soda (optional)

Combine juices with cracked ice in a
cocktail shaker. Shake vigorously. Strain
into a bamboo-style highball glass, half-
filled with crushed ice. Top up with a
little club soda if desired. Garnish with
a sprig of bamboo.

Gazpacho X

6fl oz US/180ml tomato juice
1 inch/2.5cm piece of cucumber, peeled,
   seeds removed
1 inch/2.5cm piece of celery
1 small roasted red pepper
Small pinch of dried chili flakes
Dash of freshly squeezed lemon juice

Combine ingredients in a blender with 4 or 5 ice cubes. Blend until smooth, and pour into a highball or Collins glass, half-filled with ice. Garnish with a celery stick, cucumber slices, basil leaves, and a cherry tomato.

Freeze basil leaves in the ice cubes for extra flavor and effect.

Mint Haze

2 teaspoons sugar
5 mint leaves
Dash of freshly squeezed lime juice
Sparkling apple juice

Crush the sugar and mint leaves in a pestle and mortar. Frost the rim of an old-fashioned glass by dipping it in water then in the mint sugar. Put a little more mint sugar in the glass, with three or four ice cubes. Add a dash of lime juice, then top up with sparkling apple juice.

Freeze mint leaves in the ice cubes for extra flavor and effect.

Strawberry Balsamico

5 fresh ripe strawberries
½ part sugar syrup
Dash of balsamic vinegar
Freshly ground black pepper

Combine the strawberries with the sugar syrup and four ice cubes in a blender. Blend until puréed. Pour into a highball glass filled with ice cubes. Add a dash of balsamic vinegar and a grind of black pepper. Garnish with a basil leaf and a strawberry.

Freeze basil leaves in the ice cubes for extra flavor and effect.

Grapevine

Small bunch of frozen grapes
3 parts grape juice
Bitter lemon soda

Put the frozen grapes into a chilled goblet. Pour in the grape juice, top up with bitter lemon soda, and serve straight up.

A HOUSEWIFE SMILES AS SHE STANDS AT HER FREEZER, REMOVING HALF-MOON SHAPED ICE-CUBES FROM AN AUTOMATIC ICE MAKER, AND PUTTING THEM IN GLASSES (CIRCA 1945).

Iced Tea Dance

3fl oz US/100ml cooled fruit tea (made with
  one teabag)
Sprite or 7-up
Segments of tangerine frozen in ice cubes

Pour the cold "tea" into a chilled toddy glass, and
add four decorated ice cubes. Top up with Sprite
or 7-up.

Melon Mirage

A wedge of watermelon (about one-eighth of a melon)
1 slice fresh pineapple
1 part sugar syrup
Dash of freshly squeezed lime juice

Cut two small wedges from the wedge of watermelon and a wedge out of the pineapple slice, and set aside for garnish. Peel the watermelon, remove the seeds, and peel the pineapple and remove the core. Put the fruit in a blender with crushed ice. Blend until almost smooth, adding sugar syrup and a dash of lime juice to make a pink, frothy mixture. Pour into a chilled highball glass. Garnish with watermelon and pineapple wedges and a pineapple leaf.

Cool Dude

1 part freshly squeezed lime juice
7-up
Slices of lime and lemon frozen
  in ice cubes

Pour the lime juice into an old-fashioned glass half-filled with the decorated ice cubes. Top up with 7-up and stir well.

Cranberry Grove

2 parts cranberry juice
Dash of freshly squeezed lemon
 juice
Orange soda or ginger ale

Pour the juice into a highball glass, half-filled with ice cubes, then top up with orange soda or ginger ale. Garnish with slices of orange and lemon.

Index